DOG OWNER'S GUIDE TO THE
Rottweiler

Mary Macphail

FIREFLY BOOKS

A FIREFLY BOOK

Published by Firefly Books Ltd. 2005

First printing

Publisher Cataloging-in-Publication Data (U.S.)

Macphail, Mary

   Rottweiler/Mary Macphail.

[80] p. : col. photos. ; cm. (Dog owner's guide)

Summary: A dog owner's guide to the care and training of the Rottweiler dog.

ISBN 1-55407-095-3

1. Rottweiler dog. I. Title. II. Series.

636.7/3 22 SF429.R7M33 2005

Library and Archives Canada Cataloguing in Publication

Macphail, Mary

   Rottweiler/Mary Macphail. (Dog owner's guide)

ISBN 1-55407-095-3

1. Rottweiler dog. I. Title. II. Series.

SF429.R7M33 2005 636.73 C2005-900980-2

Published in the United States by Firefly Books (U.S.) Inc. P.O. Box 1338, Ellicott Station Buffalo, New York 14205

Published in Canada by Firefly Books Ltd. 66 Leek Crescent Richmond Hill, Ontario L4B 1H1

Printed in China

ACKNOWLEDGEMENTS

I want to express my thanks to the many people who have helped me with this book with suggestions, photographs, and lending support. Alas, it is not possible to mention them all, but special thanks must go to Roy Hunter, Hilary Jupp, Elizabeth Kershaw and Liz Harrap for suggestions on the text, and to John and Ruth Gregory for providing dogs to be photographed.

CONTENTS

1 INTRODUCING THE ROTTWEILER 6

International fame; Breed characteristics (physical strength; learning ability); Owner responsibilities; Is a Rottie right for you?; Family dog; Will you be the pack leader?; Understanding the Rottie; The ideal Rottweiler.

2 FINDING A PUPPY 16

Locating a breeder; Male or female? (male traits; female traits); Assessing a litter; Health checks; What to look for; Questions & Answers; After-Sales Service; Paperwork; Words of warning.

3 THE EARLY DAYS 24

Great crates; Toys; Feeding and feeding dishes; Collecting your puppy; Housebreaking; Exercise.

4 FEEDING GUIDELINES 32

Choosing a diet; Dietary requirements (traditional; complete; changing diets); Treats.

BREED CHARACTERISTICS

For those people who understand and appreciate a highly intelligent dog, with marked guarding instincts, who thrives on human companionship, the Rottweiler is the perfect breed.

It is special in its adaptability, its intelligence, and the capacity to form a warm bond with its family. Add to these qualities, boldness, determination, working ability, confidence and strength of will, and you have a dog whose energies and intelligence need to be specifically challenged by the owner.

The owner must understand the Rottweiler, train the dog in manners, and be the pack leader. It is very necessary for the owner to assume this role; if he or she does not, the dog will.

The Rottweiler: a noble breed with a strong guarding instinct.

PHYSICAL STRENGTH

Despite his size, the Rottie should be gentle with people.

Physically, the Rottweiler is very powerful, but this does not mean that every Rottweiler needs an owner with the build of a sumo wrestler! Many small women (including myself) number among those who achieve very successful partnerships with members of the breed.

Criticisms of stubbornness and wilfulness have sometimes been leveled and, while Rottweilers can be stubborn if an owner adopts a heavy-handed approach, those who utilize the breed's play-loving traits and make training fun, with lots of praise, do not have problems.

A physical confrontation between man and dog is counter-productive—and quite unnecessary—if the dog has been trained in a kindly way with lots of praise and play.

OWNER RESPONSIBILITIES

"A dog is for life, not just for Christmas" is a slogan well known to dog lovers. But today's society is a throwaway one demanding rapid satisfaction, or else the replacement of the unsatisfactory object. Dog ownership is changing radically, and everywhere there is a marked decline in tolerance towards dogs. Stiff legislation has been introduced to ensure conformity to the public demand for a well-behaved dog which fits into an increasingly complex society.

LEARNING ABILITY

As a working dog, the Rottweiler has an excellent nose, which makes him an effective search and tracking dog. The Rottweiler is agile and quick to learn, and he possesses sufficient protective instincts that make it unnecessary to "train" a dog to guard.

However, the age at which these instincts are first manifested varies from dog to dog, and it is unrealistic to expect young puppies to guard—although some new owners are disappointed when they do not!

Guarding is an innate instinct in the breed, but it is not always evident in young pups.

IS A ROTTIE RIGHT FOR YOU?

In recent years the Rottweiler has attracted much attention, and the breed's popularity has meant that many owners have rushed out to buy one without considering the implications of owning a sizeable dog of strong character.

Dogs measure up to 27 inches (67.5 cm) at the shoulder, and bitches up to 25 inches (62.5 cm); the breed is sturdily built, with weights ranging from about 80–120 lb (36–55 kg), although specimens that are outside this range may be found.

Not surprisingly, most people view Rottweilers as large dogs and, for their size, they are extremely powerful and active, requiring a moderate amount of exercise. Therefore, if you live in an apartment, it is feasible to

Think carefully before you take on the responsibility of owning a big, powerful Rottweiler.

simple commands and aggression towards other dogs or people. Not all of us are suited to riding a mettlesome, thoroughbred horse and, in the same way, some people are much more suited to owning one of the gentler breeds.

If you intend to own a Rottweiler, you must be responsible for bringing him up to be sufficiently well behaved so that the dog fits into today's society and is a pleasant companion to his owners.

UNDERSTANDING THE ROTTIE

The Austrian writer, Adolf Ringer, gives a most apt description of the breed, which highlights the essentials of the Rottweiler's character:

"He does not tolerate being pushed here and there. He has to know where he belongs and then commits himself without qualification.

"He reacts with defiance and stubbornness to loud shouting and domineering behavior on the part of his handler or family members. He behaves in a friendly way towards children, but does not put up with being tormented.

"He ... is a dog of sound character, quiet and calm, and not upset by trifles. Nevertheless, he is always watchful and vigilant."

The Rottweiler is a dog of sound character, not upset by trifles.

The Breed Standard is a written blueprint of what the ideal Rottweiler should look like in terms of conformation, character and coat. It also describes the way a Rottweiler should move. When a dog is judged at a show, it is the individual who conforms as closely as possible to the Breed Standard that will win.

GENERAL CHARACTERISTICS

The Rottweiler is a powerful, noble-looking dog of medium size. He is capable of great strength, endurance and agility.

TEMPERAMENT

Confident and self-assured, the Rottweiler has strong guarding instincts.

HEAD

The medium length head is broad between the ears. The eyes are dark and almond-shaped. The ears are triangular and set wide apart. The teeth meet in a scissor-bite where the upper teeth closely overlap the lower teeth.

The lips are dark and firm.

THE IDEAL ROTTWEILER

FOREQUARTERS

The neck is strong and muscular, and is slightly arched. The shoulders are long and sloping, and well-laid back. The legs are straight and muscular.

BODY

The chest is broad and deep, with plenty of heart and lung room. The back is straight and slightly longer than the height of the dog.

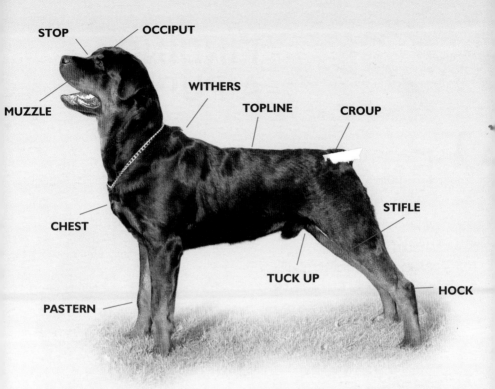

STOP

OCCIPUT

MUZZLE

WITHERS

TOPLINE

CROUP

STIFLE

CHEST

TUCK UP

HOCK

PASTERN

HINDQUARTERS
The upper and lower thighs are strong and muscular. The hindlegs, viewed from the rear, are straight and strong.

TAIL
Traditionally, the Rottweiler's tail is docked, but this is now optional.

MOVEMENT
The Rottweiler should cover the ground effortlessly, showing strength and endurance.

COAT AND COLOR
The top coat is straight, flat and coarse. The Rottweiler is predominantly black with clearly defined tan markings.

SIZE
Dogs should measure approx 25–27 in (63–69 cm) at the shoulder; bitches 23–25 in (58–63.5 cm).

2 FINDING A PUPPY

Finding a Rottweiler puppy implies a degree of search, and this is exactly what the potential owner should do.

Seek out the puppy from a litter that looks best suited to your particular needs—and this may well not appear in the first litter seen. All puppies are extremely appealing and difficult to resist, but the head should rule the heart when making this important choice.

LOCATING A BREEDER

There are many advertisements of puppies for sale in the specialist dog papers and magazines, and it is always tempting to go for the breeder that is nearest your home, or the one that has puppies that are instantly ready to go.

However, it is important to bear in mind that you are taking on a new member of the family, who will hopefully live with you for the next decade or more.

So it pays to take your time in finding the right breeder.

Your national kennel club keeps details of all Rottweiler breed clubs and, if you contact the secretary of one of the clubs, they will be able to put you in touch with some reputable breeders. If you know someone who already owns a Rottweiler, they may also be able to help you.

MALE OR FEMALE?

Before setting out to view litters, the first decision to make is whether to have a dog or a bitch. It may be that there is already a dog in the household, and so there are specific reasons why you opt for male or female. However, there are certain factors that merit careful consideration.

MALE TRAITS

Apart from being larger and stronger, the Rottweiler male has a more forceful and dominant character than the female (who rarely wants to be "leader of the pack"). A male needs an owner who understands canine mentality, who is prepared to undertake training in manners, and who is not soft or weak-willed.

If the dog is allowed to follow his own desires, with no discipline instilled in him by his owners, he will grow into an unpleasant, obnoxious animal, who will be a nuisance to all.

In an extreme case, this type of dog could end up with a one-way ticket to the veterinarian—a sad and needless waste of life.

FEMALE TRAITS

The fact that a bitch goes into heat about twice a year often deters people from owning one, associating this period with mess, hassle, and hordes of dogs clamoring at the gates. It need be none of these things. Most bitches will keep themselves pretty clean at this time, and the "danger" time when the bitch is attractive to males is only a few

A bitch is often better suited to a first-time owner.

days of her heat. (The heat lasts for a total of 21 days.)

A bitch may be spayed after her first heat, or she may be given shots to stop her going into heat. The pros and cons of both methods should be discussed with your vet.

Rottweiler bitches are usually more gentle and affectionate than the males, and they are more amenable in temperament. In fact, many breeders will not sell a male to a first-time owner, suggesting that they start off with a bitch and go for a male at a later point, when they have more experience with the breed.

ASSESSING A LITTER

When you visit a kennel or a breeder's home, make sure that the premises where the puppies are kept are scrupulously clean and odor-free.

It is important to see the mother. She should be friendly —not necessarily effusive, but certainly approachable. A nervous or aggressive mother will influence the behavior of the litter in a negative way, whereas a friendly, outgoing bitch will have a beneficial effect on her puppies.

If it is possible, try to see the father of the litter as well, even if it means making a special visit to another kennel. Again, he should be of a friendly and steady disposition.

The dam should be friendly and confident.

HEALTH CHECKS

Both parents should have had their hips x-rayed. Preferably their eyes and elbows should be checked too. It is not feasible to x-ray puppies of 7 to 8 weeks, as their joints are not fully developed but, if both parents are sound, there is a good chance that they will produce sound stock.

WHAT TO LOOK FOR

The puppies should be clean, active and friendly, with shining coats and bright eyes. They should not be fat, just nicely covered. Try not to visit the litter immediately after a meal for they will tend to be sleepy and lethargic.

Rottweiler puppies are usually very outgoing little creatures and, while your sympathy may be engaged by a rather retiring, solitary puppy who appears a little shy, do not select that one. Such a puppy will pose many problems for the new owner.

Regardless of whether puppies are reared in a commercial kennel, or are bred in a private home, it is pivotal to their mental well-being that they have contact with

Look for a bold, confident pup who comes out to greet you.

people. This is an aspect of buying a puppy that is sometimes not given sufficient emphasis, but it is crucial.

This is where a litter raised in the home can enjoy considerable advantages over puppies reared in a kennel, where it is much harder to provide the stimulation of being with people and the experience of new sights and sounds.

QUESTIONS   & ANSWERS

The breeder will be anxious to learn as much as possible about the buyer before agreeing to sell a puppy, so you should be prepared to answer some pretty searching questions before the sale goes through. He or she will want to know about your experience with dogs, the size of your house, whether you have a yard, the size of your family, whether you go out to work and whether you are willing to attend training classes with your dog. Don't be offended. All caring breeders want to be sure their puppies are going to good homes.

AFTER-SALES SERVICE

Every responsible breeder must be prepared to give "after-sales service"; the sale of a puppy does not end at the point where the buyer hands over the purchase price. Breeders should retain a lifelong interest in all their stock, and many ask to be given the chance to re-home the puppy or dog if the owner has to part with him at any time in the future.

PAPERWORK

The breeder should give you as much inform-ation as possible about the litter and the parents.

Make sure you receive a vaccination certificate, records of deworming, tattooing or microchipping, and transfer of ownership (if applicable).

In the United States, the breeder obtains a "Blue Slip" for each puppy from the American Kennel Club (AKC); the new owner then sends if to the AKC in return for a full registration certificate. In Canada, the breeder receives a registration certificate from the Canadian Kennel Club (CKC) which is then forwarded to the new owner.

The breeder should be available to give advice after the sale.

WORDS OF WARNING ...

There is a tendency, particularly with first-time buyers, to think that if they buy two puppies from the same litter, they will be company for each other. Regardless of which sex you choose, this is a mistake.

Two puppies demand an enormous investment of time and energy on the part of the owner and, to achieve their full potential, each puppy needs to have daily, individual attention and training, away from his companion. This should be for at least 15 minutes every day, longer if possible.

Battles

If the puppies are of the same sex, as they reach adolescence there may well be battles to decide which one is dominant.

No owner wants to be confronted with the task of trying to separate two young, strong Rottweilers who are intent on having a serious set-to. It is far better to start with one puppy; concentrate on the training so

Never be tempted to take on more than one puppy at a time.

that you have a well-behaved, well-adjusted adult, and then acquire a companion, preferably of the opposite sex.

23

3 THE EARLY DAYS

Preparations for your puppy's homecoming need to be made well in advance of collection, to ensure the smoothest possible transition from nest to new owner.

Decide where your puppy is going to sleep, what type of bed to use, and who is going to be responsible for feeding and exercise.

It is infinitely preferable that a puppy lives indoors as part of the family. In this way, he quickly becomes accustomed to the ways of the household, so commencing his training.

However, it is an undeniable fact that Rottweiler puppies have strong teeth, and they use them on a whole variety of objects, forbidden or otherwise. If anything "interesting" is within

reach, the puppy will investigate its durability, so, before collecting your pup, have a quick look around the house to make sure there are no objects he can grab.

If your Rottweiler is subsequently found with a precious shoe or pair of gloves, it is the owner's fault for leaving them in an accessible place!

GREAT CRATES

There are various types of beds available, such as baskets, plastic beds, beanbags and filled blankets. But for a puppy with a propensity to chew, it is an unnecessary expense to buy one of these.

The best solution is to have a collapsible indoor kennel or crate which has a removable floor of plastic or metal.

Cover this with layers of newspaper, topped with a blanket or a fleecy, washable type of bedding.

This method of housing, correctly carried out, has various benefits:

● It is an easy way of house-breaking your pup (see page 28).

● It gives the puppy a den of his own to retire to and rest undisturbed.

● It provides a way of keeping your puppy secure, and prevents chewing when the owner is not present.

Although crates are not cheap, they last a lifetime, and it is advisable to buy a size large enough to accommodate an adult Rottweiler.

The crate is collapsible so it can be taken in the car and used in a hotel bedroom (this is often a stipulation of the management, when the dog is left unattended).

Your pup will learn to look on his crate as his own special den.

DON'T FORGET THE TOYS

All puppies chew, particularly during teething at about 12 weeks, when the milk teeth are replaced by the permanent teeth. During this period it is useful to have hard chew toys available. The safest toys are made of hard rubber, available from pet stores in the form of rings, bones, etc. Aged, tough jeans, torn into strips and knotted, also provide lots of entertainment.

FEEDING AND FEEDING DISHES

Before bringing your puppy home, ask the breeder for a diet sheet to cover development to adulthood, and ensure you have a supply of the food in stock.

The diet must only be changed gradually, otherwise the puppy will suffer an upset stomach.

Food and water bowls should be made of stainless steel.

Plastic bowls are cheaper, but they are eminently chewable, and pieces could lodge in your puppy's throat. Earthenware bowls tend to crack rather easily.

In the case of heavy, rapidly growing Rottweiler puppies, it is a good idea to have the feeding dish on a stand, thus avoiding any strain on young, immature muscles and ligaments.

COLLECTING YOUR PUPPY

When the great day comes, make sure your puppy is not fed before the journey, to avoid the risk of car sickness. If possible, take another adult with you to drive the car, leaving you free to look after the puppy.

Some new owners like to have the puppy sitting on their knees on a blanket or a towel, while others prefer the puppy to be in the back of a station wagon or in a crate.

Whatever the method adopted, remember that this is the most traumatic experience your puppy will have had, and he will need reassurance to deal with the bewildering new world.

In case the puppy drools or is sick, take tissues or paper, together with a large plastic bag to use for the garbage.

When you arrive home, do not let other adults or children overwhelm the puppy. Let the pup explore, keeping you in view all the time. An hour or so after arrival, offer him something to eat. This should be exactly the same meal as the breeder would have provided. Clean water should always be available, and this should be changed several times a day.

When you arrive home, let the puppy explore his new surroundings.

HOUSEBREAKING

Young puppies need to eliminate much more frequently than adults because of their limited bladder capacity.

Select a toilet area in the yard and always take the puppy to that place. Use a command such as "Be quick," and allow time for the pup to sniff around the area. Always praise him lavishly when your puppy has performed!

At first he will have absolutely no idea what you mean but, by constantly repeating the same command, he will catch on quickly. Never correct a puppy for making a mess in the house unless you actually catch him in the act. The puppy will not associate the past action with your displeasure.

However, if you do come upon

The pup should be taken to a toileting area regularly.

the pup transgressing, utter a stern "Ahhh" and take him outside to the toilet area. In the early days of housebreaking, the watchword is vigilance.

GOLDEN RULES

Take your puppy outside at the following times:

- every time he wakes up,
- after eating or drinking,
- after playing,
- if you see him sniffing the ground and circling.

USE THE CRATE AS AN AID TO TRAINING

Puppies do not like soiling their sleeping quarters, so the business of housebreaking is accelerated if a crate is used. Initially, when the puppy needs to eliminate frequently (e.g., overnight), he will use one end of the crate, hence the need for a newspaper base, with a blanket at the other end.

A puppy may be upset when first confined to a crate, but persevere; in time, all puppies get accustomed to this "den" and will readily go in and stay there, even when the door is left open.

A young puppy should never be confined to his crate for long periods—no more than 45 minutes—except overnight.

Put your puppy in his crate for a rest after a meal, after hectic periods of playing, when you are out of the room to ensure that valuable objects cannot be chewed and, of course, at night. Never put your puppy in the crate as a punishment.

One great advantage of a collapsible crate is that it can be taken from room to room so that your pup can be with you as much as possible, under controlled circumstances.

A pup will keep his sleeping quarters clean.

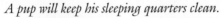

EXERCISE

A young, fast-growing, heavy Rottweiler puppy is very vulnerable to stresses and strains.

- Do not allow your puppy to go up and down stairs. The puppy should be prevented from doing this, or carried.

- Do not let your puppy climb or jump into or out of cars. He must be lifted in and out.

- Do not allow your puppy to play with other dogs without supervision and, even then, only for a very short period. Experience with the breed has shown that much damage can be done to a puppy if he is allowed to play roughly with an older dog.

- Do not exercise your puppy during the hottest part of the day in very warm weather. Restrict the puppy's exercise while he is small and ensure he has plenty of rest.

When your puppy is about 3 months old, start by taking

Exercise should be limited during the vulnerable growing period.

him for 200– to 300–yard (180– to 275–m) walks on the lead. This distance can be built up gradually. By the time your Rottweiler is 10–12 months old, you can be doing walks of about half a mile (0.8 km). Do not be tempted to let your dog jump until he is at least 18 months old.

Free-running exercise is good for a dog, but make sure that the area is suitable, such as a field, a park or a beach (but not at peak visiting hours!), and that your Rottweiler is utterly reliable at coming when called. People will be frightened by a large black-and-tan dog hurtling towards them at full tilt.

If your puppy or adult is lame, and the condition persists beyond a few days, you must have him checked by the vet.

At the first signs of lameness, rest your dog, only allowing him into the yard on a leash for toileting purposes.

FOOTNOTE

While puppies are fascinating little creatures, they can also be very trying: when unsupervised they can get into all sorts of mischief which, for them, is good, healthy fun! Their natural inquisitiveness, activity level, and propensity to chew highlight the need for the owner to institute a consistent and careful system of training. The ultimate aim is to have a puppy who easily fits into his environment, and is a pleasure to own.

4 FEEDING GUIDELINES

Establishing a good feeding regime is essential to the health and well-being of your Rottweiler. This can best be done by observing some important guidelines:

- Establish a regime from the outset, and always feed in the same place and at the same time.
- All food should be fed at room temperature; meals should not be served cold, straight from the refrigerator, or hot from a saucepan.
- Food should be prepared as near to feeding time as possible. If it is prepared too long in advance and not refrigerated, changes can take place that may adversely affect the dog.
- Food should never be kept from one meal to another. Discard any leftovers, as stale food can cause stomach upsets.
- Do not make sudden changes of diet; new food should be introduced in small quantities.
- Fresh water should always be available. If the water becomes dirty from saliva or food debris, change it.
- Never exercise immediately

before or after feeding; allow at least one hour either way.

- In very warm weather it is inadvisable to feed during the heat of the day.

- Only give marrow bones to your dog. Any other kind of bone can splinter, with dire consequences.

- A dog's food requirements differ according to age, lifestyle and state of health.

CHOOSING A DIET

There are various types of dog food on the market: complete diets that contain everything a dog needs and canned and fresh meat. Whatever you decide to feed, remember that large breeds such as the Rottweiler have a great deal of growing to do in a very short time, so a balanced diet is essential for health and growth. Rottweilers are usually very good eaters; they enjoy their food and eat with gusto. Like Oliver Twist, they always seem to ask for more! However, it is important not to overdo it, as excess weight places too much strain on developing muscles and ligaments, and a slightly lean puppy is a much healthier proposition.

DIETARY REQUIREMENTS

New owners should have received a diet sheet from the breeder which should be followed, initially at least, even if you intend to change to other foods. While exact quantities of food cannot be laid down—since each has individual requirements—frequency of feeding is as follows:

- 7–14 weeks: four meals daily.
- 4–7 months: three meals daily.
- 8 months and upwards: two meals daily.

It is better to feed an adult twice a day, morning and evening, as the dog's stomach is not then overloaded by one large meal.

Fresh drinking water should always be available.

TRADITIONAL DIET

Traditionally, a Rottweiler puppy is fed two milk-and-cereal feeds, and two meat-and-kibble feeds a day.

There is nothing wrong with this policy, and many top-class animals have been reared in this way. If you opt for a traditional method of feeding, make sure you choose good-quality meat (which will need to be minced until the pup acquires his adult teeth).

It is also recommended to add supplements in the form of sterilized bonemeal (which contains calcium and phosphorous) and cod-liver oil. It is important not to exceed the dose for supplements that is stipulated on the packaging.

As the puppy grows, the number of meals are reduced, with the aim of feeding an all-carbo-hydrates (dry kibble) breakfast and an all-meat supper by the time the dog is 12 months old.

COMPLETE DIET

Feeding methods have changed dramatically in recent times, and a complete diet is now in common use. The advantage of feeding a complete diet is that it takes all the guessing out of feeding. The manufacturers have worked out a diet with the correct balance of

THE SICK DOG

Illnesses such as kidney failure, digestive or absorption problems, diabetesmellitus, obesity and heart disease, dictate a special regime of feeding, and the owner must scrupulously follow the advice of the veterinarian.

Your Rottweiler puppy will need four meals a day when he first arrives home.

DIETARY REQUIREMENTS

carbohydrate, protein, vitamins and minerals depending on the dog's age, workload and any special needs, such as a bitch nursing a litter.

There are many complete diets available, and you will need to find the diet that suits your Rottweiler. In most cases, your puppy's breeder will have found a suitable diet, and you would be well advised to continue with this.

When you are feeding a complete diet it is important to remember that it has been correctly balanced to meet all your dog's nutritional needs. If you feed supplements, you will upset the balance of the diet. You will also need to make sure that fresh drinking water is always available.

CHANGING DIETS

If, for any reason, you need to

If you need to change diets, make the transition as gradual as possible.

change diet, make the transition from one diet to another gradual. Start by feeding a little of the new food, adding slightly more at every meal, until you have made a complete changeover. The transition from one diet to another should last over a period of days.

This will ensure your pup gets used to the new food and does not suffer an upset stomach.

GIVING TREATS

Apart from using treats as a reward when training, some owners give their Rottweilers tidbits between meals—and the dogs certainly approve! It is important to bear two points in mind: first, it is an unkindness to allow a dog to become fat, and second, do not allow your dog to solicit treats by whining, barking, drooling or looking pathetic! Let your dog earn his reward by sitting on command, carrying a small object, or in some other way gaining your approval.

It is vital to guard against obesity, as this can be the source of many health problems.

5 SOCIALIZATION AND TRAINING

S ocialization is the term used for introducing a puppy sensibly, safely and nontraumatically to all the situations he is likely to meet in his life.

This involves meeting people and other animals, and encountering different objects, sights, sounds and smells. This is a learning process that enables the dog to fit into adult life, adapting to its demands and constraints in a way that is acceptable to society, and that gives pleasure and satisfaction to the owner.

It is impossible to overestimate the importance of socialization and its influence on the mental development of any dog. It brings out a dog's full potential and in large breeds of strong character, such as Rottweilers,

German Shepherd Dogs and Dobermans, training and socialization should start from the time the puppy first arrives home.

In order to facilitate this adaptation to life through the twin routes of socialization and training, it is necessary to understand the developmental stages that all puppies go through, so that the owner may deal with situations as they arise.

STAGES OF DEVELOPMENT

Canine Socialization

Your puppy will already have reached this stage, which takes place between 4 and 7 weeks (29–49 days), when he arrives at his new home, aged 7 to 8 weeks. Prior to this, the puppy will have "learned to become a dog" by interacting with his littermates, and by learning body language and different vocalizations. Discipline is taught by the mother.

A word of warning here: never take a puppy from a breeder when he is younger than 7 weeks of age. Such puppies tend to be noisier and more prone to fighting, and they never reach their full potential. Any assurances to the contrary that a breeder might give are without foundation!

Human Socialization

This stage occurs between 7 and 12 weeks (50–84 days), and this is when you should take the time and trouble to begin training, which must be nonpunitive. Of course, puppies should have met people from the age of 3 to 4 weeks.

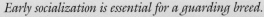

Early socialization is essential for a guarding breed.

At 8 weeks a pup is ready to absorb all new experiences.

Learning at this time is permanent and rapid, and the puppy can be taught all the commands he will need to know. Formation of attachments, "bonding" as it is termed, is at its peak at 8 weeks of age. Therefore, it is important to create a kind and sympathetic environment for the puppy.

The puppy cannot be taken out on roads and areas frequented by other dogs until his course of vaccinations is complete, but you can take him in the car for a ride (to watch other animals).

Hold the puppy in your arms, not putting him down on the sidewalk, and in this way he will become accustomed to the noise of streets, awash with people and traffic. Do not allow well-intentioned people to swoop down on your puppy, only permit carefully introduced, gentle petting.

At this time, puppies will bite in play, and you must teach bite inhibition. When your puppy nips, say "Ouch" in a sharp tone, which is usually sufficient to stop the biting. If it is not, take the puppy by the scruff of the neck, shake him, and give him a slight tap on the nose. Discipline is instant and over, as it would be given by the mother in the nest.

FEAR IMPACT

This period occurs between 8 and 11 weeks (56–77 days), and this is when any traumatic physical or mental experiences have a lasting effect. So, when you take your puppy for his shots, give him a big hug as the needle goes in, to comfort him. When it is all over, ask the veterinarian to pet your puppy and give him a treat. Beware of punitive housebreaking; the puppy can develop a fear of the person who grabs him. This is a time to protect your puppy against anything unpleasant and frightening.

This 15-week-old pup is becoming increasingly independent.

Seniority Classification

This stage occurs between 12 and 16 weeks (72–112 days) of age, when the puppy starts to "cut the apron strings" and may test for dominance. (Note: not all Rottweilers want to become the pack leader, but it is as well to know the signs.)

Play biting and mouthing must be firmly discouraged, so should biting the leash since this is regarded by the puppy as an extension of the owner's arm.

A fear stage is often experienced between 6 and 14 months.

There should be no games involving shows of strength, wrestling, tugs-of-war, etc.

The Flight Instinct

This period is of variable duration. It occurs between 4 and 8 months and corresponds to physical adolescence. The dog begins to explore the environment and may stop coming when called. Training, which should have begun earlier, takes care of this.

Fear of New Situations

This is usually related to growth spurts, and occurs between 6 and 14 months of age. Dogs will suddenly show fear of something familiar.

Do not force any dog to confront the thing that frightens

him. Remain calm and ignore your dog's reaction; do not adopt an aggressive approach or use soothing talk. The best course of action is to continue socialization and training.

Young Adulthood and Maturity

This is the final stage of development, and can occur from 12 months to 4 years; the larger the breed, the later it is. This period is characterized by the increase in size and strength, mental as well as physical.

A very dominant dog (and there are not so many of these) may renew the test for leadership. This type of dog should be treated firmly and kindly, while continuing training.

MAN–DOG RELATIONSHIP

Understanding how your dog's mind works will help you to establish a better relationship.

These critical periods have been dealt with in some detail because it is so important to the permanence and satisfaction of the man–dog relationship that the owner understands the way a dog develops.

With this knowledge, the owner can use the tools of training and socialization to deal with any problems that arise. Start training in a happy, encouraging manner from day one, bearing in mind the following points:

● A young puppy's powers of concentration are very limited,

so keep training periods short
(5–10 minutes maximum).

- Be consistent in the words
  you use when you are giving
  commands.
- Once your puppy has learned
  a command, use it only once.
- Give rewards in the form of
  tidbits and/or praise.
- Have regular play periods with
  your Rottie—both as a puppy
  and adult dog.

**There are six ways
of rewarding the puppy
(based on Roy Hunter's
Anglo-American
Dog Training):**

- **pleasant expression,**
- **posture (body),**
- **praise,**
- **pet,**
- **pop (treat),**
- **play.**

TRAINING YOUR ROTTWEILER

I have emphasized that all dogs
need some form of training to
enable them to fit into society,
otherwise problems will arise,
usually resulting in the dog being
passed on to another person or
being put down.

A Rottweiler grows very rapidly
into a large, powerful dog with a
high activity level and a strong
character, so it would be very
foolish for any owner to postpone

*Postponing lessons until your dog is
large and powerful is a big mistake.*

giving simple manners training "until the puppy is a bit older."

It is one thing to teach a young puppy to sit, lie down, and obey other basic commands, but quite another to deal with a 100–lb (45–kg) dog who does not feel particularly cooperative.

BASIC MANNERS

The time to start showing your Rottweiler what is required is from the time he first arrives home. Your puppy needs to learn:

- To come when called ("Come").
- To sit or lie down ("Sit" or "Drop").
- To stay ("Stay" or "Wait").
- To give up objects, including bones, when told ("Leave" or "Give").
- Not to pull when out on a leash ("Heel").

Allow your puppy a couple of days or so to settle in and find his way around—moving to a new home is very unsettling—then decide what words you are going to use for specific commands.

Train in a distraction-free environment so that your dog can focus on you alone.

Make training sessions fun, so that your dog wants to work with you.

Always keep to the same commands, otherwise the puppy will be totally confused. Make sure the whole family know what these commands are. Never nag the puppy; it has a depressing effect on him. When teaching your puppy any of the following exercises, initially try to do so in a distraction-free environment, such as a quiet corner of the yard or an empty room.

People moving about, noises, cooking smells and so on, will interfere with your pup's concentration.

Confident

As learning progresses and your Rottweiler matures, distractions can, and should, be introduced.

All training of young puppies must be kind, sympathetic and consistent.

Patience is vital. Puppies are very ready to learn, inquisitive and receptive to the right approach, but it must be remembered that their span of concentration is not that of an adult dog.

CRATE-TRAINING

Crate-training should begin immediately, so have the crate ready, with newspaper covered by a blanket, and let the pup investigate it. Settle on the command you intend to use, such as "Crate" or "Bed," and keep to it. Give the command, lift the puppy straight in and out, praise lavishly and give a treat. Build up time gradually and then close the crate door, but take the puppy straight out again. Next, try to coax the puppy to go in, using a treat as an incentive when he is inside, as well as giving lots of praise. Gradually build up the time your puppy is in the crate, leaving him alone in it for a few minutes while you leave the room. If a puppy is apprehensive of the crate, feed him near the crate, bringing the food bowl closer until, eventually, you are feeding the pup inside the crate. Never use the crate as punishment, and never leave the puppy in it for long periods; 45 minutes as a maximum during daylight hours, and five to six hours overnight.

COMING WHEN CALLED

It is important to remember that the dog is a pack animal, and two or more together can behave in a different, less disciplined way, however well trained they are.

Particular attention should be paid to ensuring control is maintained when more than one dog is allowed off the leash at the same time. Do not assume that you have that control; test it first in a controlled environment. This is absolutely vital.

Use a simple command like "Come," which has a staccato ring to it. Always use a light, happy tone of voice, and always make a puppy or adult feel wanted when he comes to you.

Crouch down to the level of the puppy when calling, giving lots of praise and, if you wish, a treat on arrival. Give rewards immediately, otherwise your puppy will not associate the reward with the action.

A puppy must always associate coming to the owner with pleasure, and no matter what heinous crime has been committed (in the owner's eyes), the pup must never be punished

Be ready to reward your pup when he comes to you.

when he comes. If this happens, the puppy then will come with reluctance and suspicion, if at all, and this will be to the detriment

of the relationship. It is important to teach your puppy to come when called, before he has learned to run away.

TEACHING THE SIT

If you hold a treat above your pup's head he should go into the Sit position.

Your puppy naturally knows how to sit, so it is a question of his doing this every time you ask.

To teach this, use a treat; hold it a little in front of the pup, slightly higher than eye level, then move your hand towards the back of his head and say "Sit."

Looking at the treat causes the puppy to sit, whereupon he is given the reward and praised with a "good dog."

A puppy does not always sit, so repeat the command and, with your other hand, press gently on his back just above the tail, then give the treat.

Practise this every day for about a week, with four to six repetitions at a time. Then try to get your puppy to obey with command only (rewarding him each time). Eventually, give the treat only every second or third time.

THE DOWN AND HOW TO DO IT

Use a treat to lure your puppy into the Down position.

This is an exercise to teach the dog to remain in the same position for some time, e.g., if you are having a meal, writing or have visitors.

Again, dogs know naturally how to lie down, and it is a matter of teaching your puppy to respond to the command.

To teach the command, get your puppy sitting by your left side (this is the side always used in Obedience training circles).

Hold the collar with your left hand and have a treat in your other one.

Show your puppy the treat, then lower it straight down to the floor in front of the puppy. At the same time, press gently downwards on the collar and give the command you intend to use: "Down," "Drop," or "Flat."

When your puppy lies down, praise him warmly and give the treat.

The Stay exercise has many very practical applications, and once the pup knows the exercises already discussed, he can be taught to stay in one place for increasing lengths of time.

The exercise can be started by having your puppy sit by a door and allowed to go through after about 15 seconds, when the owner says "Okay" or "Right." You can also get your puppy to sit and wait a few seconds before being given his food, before getting into or out of the car, at the side of the road and before being petted.

Do not permit the puppy to decide to get up when he wants; you must give the release command "Okay." If your puppy moves, put him back in the sit position. Your puppy should not be expected to remain in the sit position for more than a minute.

TEACHING YOUR ROTTIE TO STAY

It is not advisable to try to teach the Stay first thing in the morning, after the puppy has been asleep or in his crate, as he will be feeling very energetic and disinclined to keep still. Once the puppy lies down on command, select a place and give the command "Stay." It is helpful for the owner to have a chair or stool to sit on! If the puppy attempts

Build up the Stay exercise in easy stages.

to get up, put him down again and repeat the exercise until he stays.

To begin with, have the puppy stay for a minute, then praise and release with an "Okay." Practice, increasing the time slowly. Remember: only allow the puppy to get up when you give the release command.

With a very lively and active puppy, you can use a leash to prevent him running off.

If your puppy moves, always go back to him, never call him to you.

COLLAR AND LEASH TRAINING

Accustom your puppy to a collar (with a name/address tag) when he first arrives home. There are various types of collars available, and for daily wear a leather one with a buckle is recommended.

For training, use an adjustable collar and ensure that it fits right up behind the ears. Use a webbing or narrow leather leash, 5–6 feet (1.5–1.85 m) long. Do not use a chain or half-chain leash, as these are painful to

Encourage your pup with a toy or treat.

hold. After the puppy has become familiar with the collar, attach the leash and allow him to walk around in the home environment with the leash dragging along. This should be done only under supervision as the leash might become entangled.

When the puppy accepts this, you should take up the end of the leash and just follow him around. Next, introduce directional control, first offering treats to get the puppy to follow, then using the leash for guidance.

Exhausting

To introduce walking on the leash and to stop the puppy from pulling, which is most exhausting and irritating for the owner, seek a distraction-free area and position your puppy on your left.

Give a command such as "Heel," and start to walk in a large circle. If the puppy pulls ahead, stand still and guide him back to your side.

Repeat the command "Heel," giving a treat when the puppy returns to your side. Start with

Give lots of praise when your pup walks alongside you.

small goals in mind—just a few steps without the puppy pulling—then gradually increase the distance.

6 UNDESIRABLE BEHAVIOR

D espite training, sometimes problems do develop, and these need to be identified quickly so that measures to cure them may be taken.

In my experience, I have found the most common problems are dogs not coming when called, excessive barking, destructive behavior and aggression towards other dogs and/or people.

NOT COMING WHEN CALLED

The Recall, or coming when called, is a must and, if the foundations are well laid (see Chapter 5), this problem should not arise.

However, if it does occur, the owner must go back to basics. Put your puppy or dog on a long line (about 12 feet/3.5 m) and practice calling him to you:

"Rover, Come" (one command only), and give a quick tug on line. Reward him with a treat and lots of praise. Practice this again and again, in different places with different distractions.

When the dog is reliable, the next step is to leave the line trailing, but make sure you are in a position to take hold of the end of the line before you call your dog so he cannot make a mistake! Do not be in a hurry to take the line off; wait until you consider your dog dependable.

Now take your Rottweiler to an enclosed area where he cannot run away, remove the line and, after a few minutes, call your dog to you (one command). If your dog comes, give him praise and a reward; if not, go back to using the line. Do not expect success overnight!

Start by working on the Recall in a confined area. Progress to calling your dog at intervals when you are out walking.

Reluctance

When you are out on a walk with your Rottweiler off-leash, avoid the pitfall of calling him to you near the end of the walk to put him back on the leash. A dog will soon become wise to this, and will very likely show increasing reluctance to come.

Instead, call your dog to you several times during the walk, without putting him on the leash, and praise him before letting him run freely again. This means the dog will not form the association: leash, end of walk, don't come.

BARKING, CHEWING AND DIGGING

While barking is a very natural activity for a dog, Rottweiler owners are fortunate in that the breed is not given to barking without good reason. They are not "yappers," so this problem does not arise very often.

Nevertheless, if a dog is left for hours on end at home while the owners work full-time, barking will occur, so a dog should not be kept under these conditions.

Puppies may sometimes dig, although I have not found Rottweiler puppies do this very often, but they can be great chewers. While teething, puppies need to chew, but there is an underlying cause in the case of an adult who does this.

Whichever of these objectionable behaviors a Rottweiler exhibits, there are some factors that are common to each one:

If your Rottie is getting plenty of varied exercise, his mind will not turn to crime.

- lack of sufficient exercise,
- isolation,
- lack of mental stimulation.

A dog may also chew in order to attract the owner's attention.

Despite the fact that a Rottweiler does not require as much exercise as some other large breeds, you are inviting problems if you confine him to an apartment or a small backyard without giving him a chance for sufficient exercise.

Retrieve games provide mental stimulation.

SEPARATION ANXIETY

Dogs are social creatures; they enjoy the company of their own kind and of humans, so lengthy periods spent on their own can cause what is known as "separation anxiety." This results in unwanted behavior. This type of anxiety may be triggered by the owner making a great fuss of the dog when leaving the house. The dog, in a mood of excitement, is left alone and chews, barks, or demolishes! To avoid generating this sort of excitement, on leaving and returning to the house the owner should treat the dog in a calm, almost perfunctory manner, in order that the dog accepts comings and goings as a matter of course. The same applies when leaving the dog in a car.

MENTAL STIMULATION

A highly intelligent dog like the Rottweiler needs not only companionship, but also enough interesting, stimulating things to do to prevent the boredom which causes undesirable behavior. Not all owners play with their dogs and, by play, I do not mean roughhousing.

This type of "play" is not a good idea at all; it arouses prey instincts and may encourage the dog to become too boisterous.

Damage

Never forget that, when full grown, the Rottweiler is a very strong dog indeed. That amount of power hurtling towards you at ten miles an hour or more can cause quite a lot of damage!

Suitable games that the owner and dog may play together include retrieving objects, finding hidden objects, seeking the (hidden) owner or a friend and carrying things like the newspaper or a

The intelligent Rottweiler enjoys the challenge of learning something new.

suitable shopping basket.

Do not forget that playing games gives your dog an interest and increases the bond between you.

Some Rottweilers, usually males, can be aggressive towards other dogs. This is an unpleasant habit that needs to be stopped when first manifested.

Many training clubs run classes for puppies so that the pups can get used to other people and other dogs, and the puppies can all play together off leash.

However, training classes are not the solution for the dog who has become aggressive towards other dogs, unless the dog is initially handled on his own, away

DEALING WITH AGGRESSION

from other dogs. This should continue on a one-to-one basis, until the instructor considers the dog is ready to be introduced gradually to the class situation. An experienced trainer is required to deal with this problem.

If little or no improvement occurs, the owner should consult a veterinarian to discuss the advisability of castration.

Early socialization will prevent aggressive behavior.

AGGRESSION TOWARDS PEOPLE

Remember that all dogs can bite. Biting most commonly occurs during early adolescence (6–8 months), when the dog reaches maturity (2–3 years) and in old age.

The owner should be aware of the times when trouble may arise, be able to understand and "read" the dog, and be able to maintain control through basic manners training and careful, continuous socialization.

Dogs have dignity that strangers must respect, and it is frequently necessary to restrict well-intentioned people who overwhelm the dog with over-enthusiastic petting. Some people, especially children, have very "heavy" hands, which the dog may resent.

The Rottweiler may be aloof with strangers, but he should never be aggressive.

DOMINANCE

In the dog's eyes, within every household there is a pack leader, who may be two- or four-legged, and it is up to the owner to ensure that he or she fills this role.

Dominant dogs do not suddenly become so. Assumption of a superior position in the household is a slow process; it occurs when a dog of strong character is allowed, through the family's ignorance, to take over as pack leader. This happens in various ways:

If your dog has become dominant, you must work at lowering his status.

- The dog may be allowed to sleep on the bed, sofa or chair, and then refuse to get down.
- The dog may demand to have his food before the family eats.
- He may go through doorways first.
- He may demand (and receive) attention whenever he solicits it.
- He may become possessive with food or toys.

All these privileges belong to a pack leader and, by allowing a dog to behave in this way, the owner is confirming the dog's superiority.

To deal with a Rottweiler puppy of strong character, who seems likely to grow into a dominant adult, the owner must ensure that discipline is

61

maintained from the start in a kindly but firm way. The puppy should not be allowed to persist in any unwanted behavior.

Stop your puppy going through doorways first by physically holding him back, always giving a command such as "Back," progressing to an arm held in front of the pup's chest, then the command only.

Sensitive

Do not feed your puppy in isolation—give the pup his food where another activity is taking place, and when another person is present. Get your puppy in the habit of earning his food by having him sit briefly before eating.

Food is a very sensitive area, and neither puppy nor adult should ever be teased or interfered with when feeding. Go to the bowl to drop a little more food in it, thus showing that the

proximity of a person is not threatening. Dogs may also become possessive over objects; to avoid this, introduce toys in a play context, with the owner always initiating play and taking away the object at the end of the session. Encourage the puppy or adult to come to you with the object, and give a treat and lavish praise when he gives it to you.

Drop a treat into his bowl so that your pup learns to accept your presence at mealtimes.

BEING HANDLED

From first arriving home, the puppy should
become accustomed to being handled. Examine his ears,
inspect his teeth, pick up his feet, and clip (or file) his nails, as
necessary. The owner should gently stroke or pat the puppy on his
head, neck, shoulders and back, as this prepares the dog for the attention
of others, including the veterinarian. There is as much character variation in
dogs as in people and, just as there are potentially dominant dogs, there are
also more diffident types who need to be handled gently and with much
encouragement to equip them for life. No two puppies are alike in
temperament. Some puppies are sensitive to noise and loud
commands are demoralizing to them, while others are body-
sensitive, upset by pressure on the collar or by rough pats.
An understanding of individual character is essential
if the owner is to bring out the best in the dog,
and to establish a rewarding
bond.

7

HEALTH CARE

Rottweilers have a life span of around 10 years; large breeds do not live as long as small breeds, alas. However, good food, regular exercise and clean, comfortable living conditions contribute to keeping your dog healthy.

GENERAL CARE

Coat Care

Rottweilers have easy-care coats, and this process is quickly over.

The ideal grooming schedule is a quick daily comb and brush. If this is not possible, aim for two to three times a week, but daily when

It is important to accustom your pup to being groomed.

your dog is shedding his coat.

My preference is to use a horse's dandy brush of natural bristle, and a small rake comb, which removes any dead hair.

Start to brush (and only brush)your Rottweiler puppy from day one.

The puppy will probably not like it at first, but persevere, as he must become accustomed to being groomed from a young age.

Nails

These should be kept short; if they are allowed to become too long they can cause the feet to splay, predisposing them to injury.

Clip the nail with guillotine-style clippers, but make sure you only remove the tip of the nail, otherwise bleeding and pain will result. Alternatively, file the nails until a small area of grey/white is visible in the center of the nail—then stop.

TOOTH CHECK

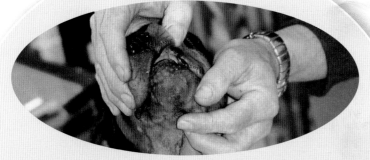

Tartar must not be allowed to accumulate on the teeth. Not only does it smell offensive, but it can also cause gum disease. If you give your Rottweiler the occasional marrow bone or hard biscuit to chew, it will help to prevent tartar forming. There are also special toothpastes and toothbrushes available for dogs.

Make sure the vet you choose is used to handling Rottweilers.

Bathing

Bathing a dog should not be done more than is absolutely necessary, as too much immersion can cause the coat to become dry.

See that the bath water is tepid only (test it by immersing your elbow), dry the dog thoroughly and, if a bath has to be given in cold weather, keep him indoors for a couple of hours to dry off thoroughly.

Choosing A Vet

Great care should be taken in your choice of veterinarian. Visit several practices to enquire about the services offered: are there any partners who specialize in small animals? Are home visits made? Are referrals to clinicians willingly given if this proves necessary?

Most important of all: is there any prejudice against Rottweilers in the practice? It does happen!

WHEN TO CONSULT YOUR VET

- If there is any rapid weight loss.
- If your Rottweiler starts to drink excessively, except in hot weather.
- If your dog's breath begins to smell strongly.
- If sickness or diarrhea lasts more than 24 hours.
- If there is bleeding from the penis, or discharge from the vulva when not in heat.
- If your Rottweiler is lame and the condition persists beyond a few days.
- If there is any marked change in behavior.

CONTAGIOUS DISEASES

Apart from the owner's contribution mentioned above, there are other factors that must be taken into account. First and foremost, every Rottweiler puppy must have a course of vaccinations to protect him against potentially lethal contagious diseases: distemper, hepatitis, parvovirus and pavainfluenza. Vaccination against leptospirosis is also recommended, in areas where the disease is endemic.

It is essential to give these booster shots throughout the life of the dog as a preventive measure.

In Canada and parts of the United States it is compulsory for dogs to be vaccinated against rabies.

The adult Rottweiler will need booster vaccinations throughout his life.

INHERITED DISEASES

Hip Dysplasia (HD)

Orthopedic problems are high on the list of conditions that affect the larger breeds.

The most common of these is HD, an inherited condition in

which the hip joint, a ball-and-socket joint, is malformed. The degree of unsoundness and discomfort depends on the extent of the malformation. In severe cases, surgical intervention may be needed in order to alleviate the pain.

It is impossible for any breeder to be certain that a puppy will not develop HD, but the chances are considerably reduced if the parents are x-rayed through an official kennel club program or some other reliable agency, and have a low score.

While HD is an inherited disease, the environment also plays a part, and no Rottweiler puppy should be allowed to become overweight, play on slippery surfaces (like tiles or polished floors), or run up and down stairs while he is growing.

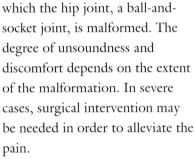

Hips must be x-rayed and scored before a dog is used for breeding.

THE FACTS ABOUT OSTEOCHONDROSIS

Osteochondrosis (OCD) is considered by some clinicians to be the most common cause of lameness in the young dog of the larger breeds. It is a disease of growing cartilage that fails to turn into bone. Cracks appear, and sometimes pieces of the joint flake off. There are varying degrees of pain and unsoundness, and the condition is found in the shoulder, elbow, hock and stifle. Rottweilers are frequently affected in the elbow.

If a puppy becomes lame, he should be rested (not always so easy!) and, if he is still lame after a week, he should be checked by a veterinarian who may refer you to a clinician for further investigation.

Surgery may be advised, depending on the severity of the condition. While there is not yet general agreement, osteochondrosis is thought to be an inherited condition.

The Rottweiler is most frequently affected by OCD in the elbow joint.

CRUCIATE LIGAMENTS

The bones of the knee (stifle joint) are held together by several cruciate ligaments, and rupture of the anterior ligament is a common problem in the heavier breeds, occurring very often in dogs under the age of 3 years.

At first, the ligament stretches, causing the knee joint to become unstable, and eventually it ruptures. The dog may not show any initial lameness, but as the ligament stretches, then ruptures, the dog will become unsound. From the time the joint becomes unstable, osteoarthritis starts to develop. If the ligament is not repaired, the arthritis worsens, so the earlier surgery is carried out, the better for the dog. After the operation, which is usually extremely successful, a most carefully controlled regime of exercise is necessary.

For approximately one month, the dog must go into the yard on leash for toileting only, then on leash for a distance of 100–300 yards (90–275 m) for a further month and, after that, the distance can be increased gradually, carefully monitoring progress. Make haste slowly is the golden rule. If the owner does not, the surgeon's work will have been in vain.

Certain bloodlines seem to be affected more than others, and dogs that have been operated on should not be bred from.

DEALING WITH EYE PROBLEMS

The most common eye disease is entropion, where the eyelid(s) turn inwards. This causes "runny" eyes, inflammation, and possibly ulceration of the cornea, which is extremely painful. While it usually occurs in dogs with a lot of loose skin on the head, this is not always so. Although entropion sometimes occurs as a secondary condition, it is usually considered to be an inherited problem, which must be referred to a veterinarian quickly. It is cruel not to have the condition corrected surgically, and this is quite a simple operation. Dogs with this problem should not be used for breeding. Should your Rottweiler develop "runny" eyes, consult a veterinarian; often, all that is needed is ointment to be applied two or three times a day for 7–10 days.

TAKE GOOD CARE OF THE SKIN

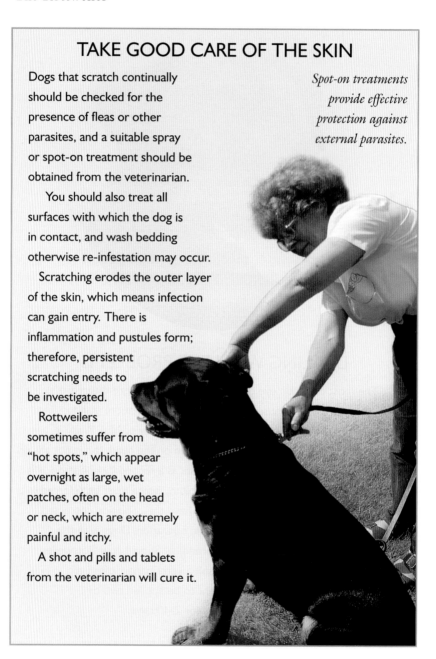

Dogs that scratch continually should be checked for the presence of fleas or other parasites, and a suitable spray or spot-on treatment should be obtained from the veterinarian.

You should also treat all surfaces with which the dog is in contact, and wash bedding otherwise re-infestation may occur.

Scratching erodes the outer layer of the skin, which means infection can gain entry. There is inflammation and pustules form; therefore, persistent scratching needs to be investigated.

Rottweilers sometimes suffer from "hot spots," which appear overnight as large, wet patches, often on the head or neck, which are extremely painful and itchy.

A shot and pills and tablets from the veterinarian will cure it.

Spot-on treatments provide effective protection against external parasites.

BLOAT AND GASTRIC TORSION

Bloat is a condition most often found in medium-sized and large, deep-bodied dogs, which usually occurs shortly after feeding when the stomach rapidly fills with gas, swelling up and sometimes also twisting (gastric torsion). The dog is in great pain, has difficulty in breathing, retches but cannot vomit, and is greatly distressed.

This is a grade-one emergency and you should telephone your veterinarian to say you are bringing the dog immediately.

Seconds Count

Even seconds may mean the difference between life and death; this condition is a killer.

Various causes are thought to contribute to this condition, such as consuming dry food followed by copious drinking, vigorous exercise too soon after a meal, food fermenting in the stomach, overloading the stomach and swallowing an abnormal amount of air, which can be the case with greedy, rapid eaters. It is most

Never exercise your Rottweiler right after he has eaten.

common in breeds such as Bloodhounds and Irish Wolfhounds, but it can occur in Rottweilers, too. It is better to check a false alarm than have the dog suffer an agonizing death.

COPING WITH CANCER

Unfortunately, cancer is far from uncommon in Rottweilers, and bone cancer (osteosarcoma) is probably the most prevalent. With the increasing sophistication of veterinary medicine, treatments such as chemotherapy and radiotherapy are available at some veterinary colleges, and techniques are improving all the time. However, some types of cancer are not amenable to treatment and there is no alternative but euthanasia.

INTERNAL PARASITES

Throughout their lives, dogs should be dewormed at regular intervals of three to six months, for the sake of the animal's health and that of his human family.

There are four main types of worms—round (the most common), hook, whip and tape—and there are preparations available from a veterinarian that will deal with all four at once. Worms are easily picked up through sniffing feces of other dogs, eating affected meat and through fleas.

Heartworm can be fatal to dogs and is endemic in parts of the United States and Canada; ask your vet to test your dog and recommend an appropriate preventive treatment.

Your Rottweiler will need to be wormed on a routine basis.

THE LAST GOODBYE

When a Rottweiler has given pleasure to his owner and family, and the sad time comes when his quality of life is no longer good, the dog should be put to sleep. Preferably in his own home, and in the owner's arms, while the owner is reassuring him. However painful this may be for the owner, it is the last kindness you can do for a loyal companion, and it is one you should never avoid.

8

When your Rottweiler grows up, there are lots of fun activities you can get involved with which will enhance your relationship with your dog.

The versatile Rottie will enjoy all training challenges that come his way.

THE CHALLENGE OF

Rottweilers are a working breed, and there are several activities for which they can be trained where they perform with credit. These events include Working Trials, Competitive Obedience and Agility.

There are clubs that specialize in these activities, and your Rottweiler

Tracking is an important element of Working Trials.

THERAPY DOGS

Research has shown that communicating with a dog has a beneficial effect on humans. Stroking dogs helps us to relax and lowers stress levels. Hospitals, nursing homes and schools for children with special needs receive visits from owners and their dogs. Many elderly, long-stay patients have had to part with much-loved pets when they entered hospital and miss them badly, so the canine visitors bring back happy memories. Therapy dogs are officially assessed for suitability and Rottweilers that make visits are extremely successful: gentle with the elderly and patient with children, enjoying all the attention they receive.

WORKING EVENTS

will thrive on the challenges they provide. Anyone interested in learning more about Trials, Obedience or Agility, and where training classes are held, may obtain details from their national kennel club in the countries where these competitions are available.

Agility is a fun sport for both dog and handler.

ALL THE FUN OF THE DOG SHOW

You will need to train your Rottweiler to stand in show pose.

Dog shows are held under the auspices of the kennel clubs of various countries; dogs compete against each other, the winners being those who, in the opinion of the judge, most closely fit the Breed Standard (see page 14).

Being a popular breed, entries in Rottweiler classes are high, and an owner should seek advice from the breeder concerning the dog's chances as there is no point in wasting time and money entering shows if the dog is not of show quality.

Indeed, the owner should decide whether he or she wants to show their Rottweiler before they buy a puppy, and then go to a breeder with a proven record of success in the show ring.

If you show your dog, you will need to train him so that he can show himself off to advantage in the ring.

The dog will need to stand in a show pose, tolerate being handled by the judge, and learn to move across the ring in step with his handler.

CARTING

These events are organized in the U.S. and Canada.
The American Rottweiler Association offers three levels of carting
competition: CS Carting Started, CI Carting Intermediate and CX Carting
Excellent. Dogs also pull carts (sometimes with a passenger on board)
at parades and processions, and they always attract a lot of attention.
To find events to participate in contact your city hall,
local service clubs or dog clubs about upcoming
parades or processions.

IN CONCLUSION...

In this short book I have tried to do justice to a great breed whose qualities make him outstanding as a companion and protector of home and family, as well as a working dog.

I should like to end with the words of an American friend, who said so rightly: "A dog is not good at knowing what to do, only what he has been taught to do." Give your Rottweiler affection and kindness. Take the trouble to train and to guide him.

Your reward will be loyalty and companionship all the days of his life.

ABOUT THE AUTHOR

Mary Macphail owned her first Rottweiler in 1958 and since then she has bred, exhibited and judged the breed with great success.

She is an international Championship Show judge, and she has judged Rottweilers at Crufts on two occasions, including at the Crufts Centenary Show. Mrs. Macphail has now judged the Rottweiler in 14 different countries, including the United States, Canada, Australia, New Zealand, Norway, Holland and Israel. She has also judged the breed in Germany, and she is the only person in Britain who is qualified to judge the Rottweiler in its country of origin.

Mrs. Macphail has written for *Dog World* for the last 30 years, and has a diploma in companion animal behavior counseling from Southampton University, U.K.